Prepare Your Heart for a

Great Christmas

*Prepare Your Heart (and home) for a
Great Christmas this year!*

Visit **www.GreatChristmasBook.com** for your free
7-Step Action Plan for a Great Christmas, written
by Julie Hood, author of the best-selling e-book
The Organized Writer and Fortune 500 consultant.

Prepare Your Heart for a
Great Christmas

By: Maria Rodgers O'Rourke

MRO Communications, Inc., Publisher

To my mother, who taught me to love Christmas.

Preface

The holidays come with romantic ideas of evenings by the fire, reading special Christmas books, baking cookies, singing carols, and exchanging gifts while snowflakes gently fall outside the window. These ideal Christmas scenes don't often match the reality of what it takes to create them, and mom is usually the one responsible for getting it all done.

This book is for all women who want to prepare for December 25th in the true Christmas spirit, and to enjoy the season with her mind, heart and soul intact!

During the holiday season, already busy lives are loaded with more tasks, parties, special services at church, gifts to buy, folks to remember, etc. Through daily prayer, gratitude and intention, we meet these demands with greater peace and humor. When entrusted to God, the challenges of daily life come into proper perspective.

Our understanding of Advent (with a capital "A") means the time in preparation for Christmas. In addition to this, advent means coming into vision, time or being. Our efforts will bring into being wonderful Christmas and holiday celebrations. By holding these efforts in the context of gratitude and prayer, we will experience greater peace throughout the season. Our joy and gratitude will spread to those around us. Thus, both Advent and advent preparations are essential for you and those you love.

Give yourself the gift of a great Christmas by taking quiet time everyday. The spirit of Christmas is alive and ready to fill your life with joy and blessings. Follow this book's simple formula and prepare your heart for a great Christmas.

How to Prepare Your Heart for a Great Christmas:

The reflections begin on Thanksgiving Day, followed by a series of reflections (entitled Thanksgiving Season) to finish out the month of November. Read and follow as many as needed to bring you to December 1. Then, the reflections and journal pages follow the calendar dates through January 1. The Christmas Season reflections follow until the Feast of the Epiphany, celebrated in many churches as the visit of the Magi to the infant Jesus.

Each day, find a quiet place and take a few deep breaths. Read the day's reflection, and ponder the words and phrases that strike you. Then, turn to the facing journal page and answer the questions listed there. The questions are the same everyday, but your answers will vary. Here are some examples:

- Today I am grateful for … (A simple list will do: my home, my health, a warm cup of coffee, sunshine.)

- My intention for today … (Example: to appreciate my child's energy; to be kind to all whom I meet; to be patient in traffic)

- My to-do list for today includes … (whatever tasks you have on your mind or need to accomplish.)

This book is your book; go ahead and write in it! Carry it with you throughout the day, crossing off your to-do list and rereading your gratitude list and intention statement. Extra journal pages for your thoughts and ideas are included in the back of the book. Use this book to remember the reasons why you're doing what you're doing, and God's constant companionship throughout the day.

Thanksgiving Day

Give thanks to the Lord, for he is good.
Daniel 3:89

The great prayer traditions teach us to begin our prayer time with praise and thanksgiving. This approach helps our souls on several levels—it focuses our attention on what's right in our world; it reminds us of our proper relationship to God and creation, and it brings instant peace in the midst of our hectic lives and busy minds.

It is appropriate to begin our holiday season on a day established for the purpose of giving thanks. We start not only the holiday season, but also this pact we've made with ourselves to take quiet time everyday and prepare our hearts for the miracle of Christmas.

As we give thanks today, we are like the pilgrims: venturing into unknown regions of our hearts, creating a new way of holiday life for our family and friends, seeking the freedom of heart to enjoy the season no matter the demands on our time, attention and energy. Ultimately, we desire the realization of the promise that only God can fulfill—a promise of peace that the world cannot take away.

As you move through your day today, pay attention to the big and little things that are meaningful to you: from the people you love, to that wonderful light in the refrigerator that comes on just when you need it. Say "Thank you!" Then give thanks for how light your heart feels after you've said those two simple, life-affirming words!

today I am grateful for _____

_____

_____

_____

my intentions for the day _____

_____

_____

_____

my to-do list for today _____

_____

_____

_____

_____

_____

_____

Thanksgiving Season

What has come into being in him was life, and the life
was the light of all people. The light shines in the darkness,
and the darkness did not overcome it.
John 1:4-5

In recent years the media has dubbed the day after Thanksgiving "Black Friday." Retailers hope for a successful shopping day to kick off the industry's most lucrative time of the year. Black Friday is a fitting name in the retail world and the natural world as well. Many shoppers begin their preparations in the dark, either pre-dawn or earlier, and this time of year includes the longest nights and darkest days of our calendar.

Yet in this darkness, light displays twinkle in stores, parks, and on homes. The displays date back to a time when folks more closely in rhythm with the earth than we are observed the winter solstice. Christmas and Hanukkah, the "Festival of Lights," are celebrated when our hemisphere turns back toward the sun. After the darkest, longest night of the year, our world will turn and slowly reclaim the light and warmth of summer.

During Advent we anticipate the world's return to the light. Light a candle where you can see it throughout the day. Savor its warm light, and say a prayer for someone you know who needs an extra serving of grace today.

today I am grateful for _____

_____

_____

_____

my intentions for the day _____

_____

_____

_____

my to-do list for today _____

_____

_____

_____

_____

_____

Thanksgiving Season

All things work together for good for those who love God.
Romans 8:26-30

There's a lot of work that goes in to getting ready for Christmas. Whether you've been preparing for months or have barely started, the clock starts ticking this weekend. And it doesn't give you much time. There's a very special baby on the way, and you know how demanding babies are!

Before you start running to catch up, keep in mind our scripture passage, above. No matter where you are with your preparations, God's grace will work with you, right where you are. Before you give in to the weight of feeling that it all depends on you, remember that, in reality, it doesn't. God is in charge, and God will get you through.

We set our minds on an ideal of what the perfect holiday celebration will be. Maybe there are other possibilities out there, things God has dreamed for us and those we love. Those new possibilities will break through only when we step aside and let them emerge. Don't play God by trying to control everything or by pretending it all depends on you. Remember, there is a divine providence in our lives that wills great joy for you and everyone you love. Trust that providence to be big enough and generous enough to provide a great Christmas again this year. You don't have to do it alone.

today I am grateful for

my intentions for the day

my to-do list for today

Thanksgiving Season

For the sake of my relatives and friends, I will say "Peace be with you!"
Psalm 122:6-8

Music has tremendous power to affect our mood and tap into memories. Christmas music is a highlight of the holiday season for me. There are songs that take me back to my childhood, and music that brings to mind the joy of my own family at Christmas time. Each new holiday season, I'm delighted by moments when I hear an old song as if for the first time.

There's a radio station that begins playing Christmas songs on Black Friday. That station was on while I fixed dinner one night. Suddenly, my youngest daughter ran in the kitchen, giggling. She grabbed my hands and started dancing with me. As we swirled around the kitchen, the singers proclaimed their need for a little Christmas … right now.

Tears came to my eyes. With my delighted, dancing daughter beaming at me, in the midst of cooking dinner and the stress of Christmas preparations looming, I found myself in a Christmas Moment. Despite the demands the season makes, I need its music, its laughter, its promise and hope. I need a little Christmas now.

today I am grateful for

_____

_____

_____

my intentions for the day

_____

_____

_____

my to-do list for today

_____

_____

_____

_____

_____

_____

The earth is the Lord's and all that is in it.
Psalm 24:1

O ur gratitude practice helps us realize the power of this passage. All the things of this earth came from God, and belong to God. We are simply the caretakers, or stewards of creation. It is at once an awesome and terrifying charge.

Contemplate the expanse of creation as we know it in our world: the beauty of the land, the power of the sea, all the forms of life found around the world and the diversity of cultures. These inspire awe and wonder at God's creativity, resourcefulness and power.

Then think of human beings possessing the abilities of mind and will to harness the gifts of the earth, and to create new and wondrous things. With these abilities comes the responsibility to take care of the resources, and to remember, ultimately, from whence they came.

As we prepare our hearts and homes for Christmas, let's remember that all the things we worry about and fuss over really belong to God. God has entrusted them to us at this time. May we use them to give glory to their Creator.

today I am grateful for

my intentions for the day

my to-do list for today

Thanksgiving Season

The mountains and hills before you shall burst into song, and
all the trees of the field shall clap their hands.
Isaiah 55:12

We're busy these days: work demands, taking care of the kids, running errands, preparing for Christmas. The pace is overwhelming. We move so quickly from one thing to the next that some days are just a blur of activity, people and tasks.

But for the last few days, we've created a haven of quiet and peace with our daily reflection and journaling time. Has the gratitude practice started to take effect? Have you noticed some things around you, that maybe in the past you might have been too busy to note? Like how the sunlight comes in through the kitchen window in the morning, or how a song you love comes on the radio just when you need a pick-me-up, or that project you were dreading turned out to be easier than you expected?

These moments of beauty are always there for our enjoyment, but we're not always paying attention! When we are grateful for the blessings we see, our eyes are opened to even more.

Perhaps your gratitude list has gotten repetitious these days. Take an extra minute or two to come up with some new items for the list, no matter how insignificant you may think they are.

today I am grateful for _____

_____

_____

_____

my intentions for the day _____

_____

_____

_____

my to-do list for today _____

_____

_____

_____

_____

_____

_____

_____

> *Be on guard so that your hearts are not weighed*
> *down with the worries of this life.*
> Luke 21:34

As I look around the world, I see a lot of changes to be made. Conflict and strife, waste, hunger and fear … and that's just in my own family! There's so much we see and dream "if only" it were different: if only we could get through this challenge, if only everyone else saw things the same way we do.

We feel at odds with the world, yet change begins with us. We are called to truly live the Golden Rule: to treat others the way we'd like to be treated. There will be extra conflicts this time of year as we try to meet and manage the expectations of those we love. Some we will fulfill; others will be disappointed. But it all starts with us—how connected are we to God, the great source of love, compassion and reconciliation? The more connected we are, the more our presence and efforts will give witness to God's love.

When you wonder, "if only …," take a deep breath. Get your bearings. Open your heart to the creative love of God, and watch the changes come.

today I am grateful for _____

_____

_____

my intentions for the day _____

_____

_____

_____

my to-do list for today _____

_____

_____

_____

_____

_____

_____

*I, John, saw another angel coming down from the heaven, having great
authority; and the earth was made bright with his splendor.
Revelation 18:1*

One of my kids' all-time favorite movies is *Angels in the Outfield*.
In it, a boy named Roger is the only person who can see angels
assisting the professional baseball team of the same name. The first
ones Roger spots appear much like the angel John saw—swooping
down from the heavens, their light radiating all around them—then
lifting an outfielder into the air to make a miraculous catch.

The angels appear in response to Roger's prayer, prayed less for the
baseball team than for his broken family. The celestial allies help the
Angels all the way to the big championship game. In the process
Roger's prayer is answered, though not in the way he had imagined.
When we pray, we have to be prepared to leave the answer up to God,
too.

Angels herald this great season of love—from the Annunciation of
Mary to the shepherds in the field—all the earth lighted by their glory,
carrying a message from on high. Perhaps our own angels will make an
appearance. As we pray for a special Christmas this year, may we be
blessed with the grace to accept however our prayer is answered.

today I am grateful for _____

_____

_____

my intentions for the day _____

_____

_____

my to-do list for today _____

_____

_____

_____

_____

_____

_____

Thanksgiving Season

Then I saw a new heaven and a new earth.
Revelation 21:2

I'd like some new things this season: new clothes, new books, gifts thoughtfully chosen just for me. (It is all about me, isn't it?!)

We have to be careful when it comes to new things, though. If we're down, new stuff can cheer us up, but only temporarily. On a larger scale, when troubles come, our first thought may be to change the situation to something new. "I need a new job … car … house … spouse." New things are fun, but let's not trust in *stuff* to solve our problems.

The real transformation comes when we can view what we already have with new eyes: to see the inherent goodness in the people and circumstances of our lives, and to take that as the starting point for our world view. John saw creation transformed, and with eyes of faith we will see it, too.

Take a quiet walk today. Breathe deeply to clear your head and fill your lungs with fresh air. It's a mini-miracle how a quick step outside will change our perception of things.

today I am grateful for _____

_____

_____

_____

my intentions for the day _____

_____

_____

_____

my to-do list for today _____

_____

_____

_____

_____

_____

_____

> *The night is far gone; the day draws near.*
> *Romans 13:12*

Since the middle ages, the Advent Wreath has been part of Christian spiritual preparation for Christmas. This tradition emerged from an ancient practice of farmers and laborers who, having completed the season's harvest, used greenery and candles to celebrate the solstice and the coming spring.

The wreath is rich in symbolism for Advent preparations. The light is, of course, that of Jesus Christ, coming to a world so desperately in need of his perfect love. The greenery assures us that no matter the losses or challenges we face, God's life renews any situation, resurrecting that which was thought to be dead.

The wreath's circle symbolizes the Advent journey. As we've discovered in life, the attainment of wisdom and peace is not a linear journey; rather, it is a circular one. We may travel through the same issues many times in life, but when we face these issues with open hearts, we grow ever-closer to God. This month, we will journey with Mary and Joseph, the Magi, and Christians around the world and rediscover the light and life of Jesus Christ.

Light an Advent Wreath this year. Celebrate these blessed days that focus our attention on the reason for the season.

today I am grateful for My legs that I can walk & do things & can serve God unhindered.

my intentions for the day Please Lord help me in my organization of house, family & mind. I need your help to succeed & persevere

my to-do list for today
- Mom's Meeting
- order Christmas Cards
- ornaments
- junk drawer

December 2

Many will come from the east and the west and will eat with Abraham, Isaac and Jacob in the kingdom of heaven.
Matthew 8:11

Even as a baby, Jesus called followers from all walks of life and all parts of the world. Shepherds and kings were equally welcome to bask in his glory and peace.

The invitation extends over the centuries to believers today. The door is always open, the love and mercy unlimited. Every year, as we follow Advent to the feast of Christmas, we are invited again to meet Jesus, and to know him more intimately than before.

The manger scene is a powerful reminder of God's eternal open door policy. As you set up your crèche this year, reflect upon each character and the special purpose he or she had to bring Jesus into the world. Pray for an open heart to accept this year's invitation.

today I am grateful for _____

_____

_____

my intentions for the day _____

_____

_____

_____

my to-do list for today _____

_____

_____

_____

_____

_____

_____

December 3

You have hidden these things from the wise and intelligent and have revealed them to infants. Luke 10:21

Santa's days are numbered in some homes. The end is coming, and I don't mean December 25th. Children everywhere are contemplating the ultimate Christmastime question: "Is Santa real?"

How to answer this question? My own mother's response was, "Santa is love." As a second grade teacher and mother to my five older siblings and me, she was confronted with this question countless times. As a teacher, she wove the spirit of her response into relevant curriculum concepts. For example, in science lessons she explained that even the most talented heart surgeon, administering life-saving procedures to his patients, holds only the tissue in his hands. She asked her class: "Does the doctor see love, goodness, trust and happiness as he operates on the human heart?" "No," replied the class. "Do you know love, goodness, trust and happiness in your life—the most dynamic functions of the human heart?" The answer was an emphatic "Yes!"

Children know love when they see it. Our cultural images of Santa portray selfless love and thoughtful concern for others—qualities all of us, at any age, can emulate. Giving up Santa means the end of a sweet, innocent time, but the love lessons of Santa can instruct us all of our lives.

today I am grateful for _____

_____

_____

_____

my intentions for the day _____

_____

_____

_____

my to-do list for today _____

_____

_____

_____

_____

_____

_____

December 4

The Lord God will wipe away the tears from all faces.
Isaiah 25:8

My husband and I faced the "Is Santa real?" question with each of our daughters. Last year, as we decorated the tree, our youngest casually asked, "Mom, is Santa real?" My husband and I exchanged a look. Caught off guard, I replied: "What do you think?" She didn't respond. I bought some time, but knew I needed an answer very soon.

I needed more time, remembering the year our older daughter discovered the truth. On Christmas Eve she dozed on the couch, determined to prove us wrong and catch Santa Claus in the act. She's a heavy sleeper, and we managed to tip-toe around the tree while she snoozed. By the next Christmas season, she had resigned herself to Santa's legendary (not physical) state, albeit with some sadness.

I was sad, too. My husband and I knew, however, that we'd created this dilemma. We were always uneasy with misleading our trusting daughters. How could we have fostered this fantasy, all the while knowing one day we'd have to tell them otherwise?

It's good to know God's love will comfort and sustain our children, even when the best of intentions lead to disappointment and hurt feelings.

today I am grateful for

my intentions for the day

my to-do list for today

December 5

Return, O my soul, to your rest, for the Lord has dealt bountifully with you.
Psalm 116:7

Throughout her life, my mother opened my eyes to a dimension in life beyond what the hand has touched and the eye has seen. When her grandchildren began asking The Question, she wanted a more permanent record of her insights, so she wrote a Letter to the Editor of our local paper. Published on Christmas Day, it said, "Yes, my dearest child, there is a Santa Claus! You will find him not only in the packages that you unwrap, but in the greatest gift we give—the gift of ourselves to each other!"

In the end, we welcomed Santa into our home because we want our daughters to share this perspective. Life is made richer through acts of love and generosity, and by gifts freely given from the heart of the giver.

Many years ago, a new image of Santa was added to our family's Christmas decorations—a small figurine of Santa kneeling, hat in hand, before the holy child. While Santa doesn't join the gathering at the stable, this little statue does express how he fits into the Christmas story.

When feeling overwhelmed this season, remember Jesus and Santa together this way. Two great models of love, sharing a Christmas Moment.

today I am grateful for _____

_____

_____

my intentions for the day _____

_____

_____

_____

my to-do list for today _____

_____

_____

_____

_____

_____

December 6

According to your faith let it be done to you.
Matthew 9:29

The day of reckoning came. I'd dodged the issue long enough. As I prepared dinner one evening, Katie sat at the kitchen counter, stared straight into my eyes and asked: "Mom, is Santa real? Do you believe in Santa?"

I took a deep breath and searched for the words my mother told me. "Well, Katie, Santa is love. Wherever you find people being good to one another at Christmastime, Santa is there." I chose my words carefully—too slowly for my eager child. Impatient, she interrupted me and said, "Well, *I* believe in him." She stared one second longer, emphasizing her point. I smiled, gazed back and said, "I believe in him, too." Returning the smile, she hopped down and ran from the room. She had found her answer.

The legend of today's Santa Claus began with St. Nicholas. Born in the fourth century, he inherited a fortune when he was a young man. In his desire to serve the poor, Nicholas came to the aid of an impoverished family with three daughters. Under the cover of night, he delivered sacks of money to the home. In the years following his death, tales of his goodness spawned his saintly patronage of children. Families in Germany, Switzerland and the Netherlands were the first to give presents in his name at Christmastime. Ultimately his legend known as Santa Claus was popularized in America by Dutch Protestant Christians.

today I am grateful for

my intentions for the day

my to-do list for today

Do not be afraid, Zechariah. Your wife Elizabeth will bear you a son …
John. He will be great in the sight of the Lord.
Luke 1:13-15

The angel Gabriel makes one of his many Advent appearances, proclaiming to Zechariah that his prayers had been heard and answered. Yet, Zechariah, through his barrage of questions, denies the blessing and loses his voice. His fear and lack of faith plunge him into silence.

Sometimes, a bit of blind faith is what's in order. Zechariah had no idea how his blessing would come into being, and so he was convinced that it simply couldn't be done. Turning dreams into reality is God's work, though. When we ask God for something, we need to let go of the outcome, and trust that our prayers will be answered in the way that is best for us.

The good news is that God moved to fulfill Zechariah's dream. Elizabeth carried the baby, her heart filled with praise and thanks to God. When the baby was born, Zechariah named him John, and his voice returned. In the instant Zechariah embraced God's blessing he became filled with new life.

Today, be open to an unexpected blessing. Don't push it away with questions or doubts. Accept the gift. God chose it just for you. Go on, take it!

today I am grateful for

my intentions for the day

my to-do list for today

December 8

Here I am, the servant of the Lord; let it be with me according to your word.
Luke 1:38

Mary speaks the "yes" that changed the world. Mary: the first to believe.

Mary is the inspiration for all who seek to be God's instrument in their daily lives. In the midst of her life, the life chosen for her by her family, God's angel visits her to proclaim the news of her glorious vocation. She accepts. Yet, as time goes on, the details of her day-to-day life do not change dramatically. She weds Joseph (who needed some intervention of his own!) keeps house and tends the family … pretty much what she'd planned before the angel's announcement.

So it can be for believers today. God works through us right where we are, in this moment. To follow God's call, we don't have to abandon our life—a fear we may harbor. No, we're asked to give our lives to God and to allow his grace to work in and through us in our present circumstances. It is so simple a request, yet one with potentially universal consequences. Just ask the sweet girl from Nazareth.

today I am grateful for

my intentions for the day

my to-do list for today

> *Say to those who are of a fearful heart, "Be strong, do not fear!"*
> *Isaiah 35:4*

I have so much I want to do but it all gets added on top of an already full schedule and the days are speeding by and I wonder how I'll get it all done and surely I won't because how could anyone get all this done? I'm only human you know and these people just need to understand what my life is like and if they did they'd be grateful for what little they get of me since I'm so spread out in so many different directions...!

Sound familiar?

The creator of *The Incredibles* movie said in an interview that he'd based each character on a stereotypical trait reflecting their role in life. Their superhero powers sprang from this. Thus, Elasti-Girl was invented. Elasti-Girl's character is Mom, constantly pulled in opposing directions, the caretaker of the family, passionate advocate for and disciplinarian of her brood of blooming superhero children.

I feel a bond with Elasti-Girl, though my muscles would snap if stretched like that. I'm pulled in so many directions, and afraid I won't get everything done. God help me to hold it together!

today I am grateful for _____

_____

_____

_____

my intentions for the day _____

_____

_____

_____

my to-do list for today _____

_____

_____

_____

_____

_____

_____

Comfort, O comfort my people, says your God.
Isaiah 40:1

"It is one of the most beautiful compensations of this life that no man can sincerely try to help another without helping himself."
~ *Ralph Waldo Emerson*

This time of year is the season of giving: to those we love, and to strangers through the countless charities that ask for help. In giving, we count the cost, in terms of our time, energy and bank account.

Emerson offers us a different perspective from giving as a one-sided exchange. When we freely give, the goodness comes back somehow. It most often is not in the moment of giving, but at another time when unexpected kindness is shown to us.

Giving is great exercise. It stretches and opens our rigid selves to new experiences and possibilities. From networking meetings to soup kitchens, we all are part of a circle of goodness far greater than any we could quantify. Thus, it really isn't about the size of our gift, it's about giving, period.

This year, give and give generously without counting the cost. Trust that there is enough to go around.

today I am grateful for _____

_____

_____

my intentions for the day _____

_____

_____

my to-do list for today _____

_____

_____

_____

_____

_____

> *Come to me, all you that are weary and are carrying*
> *heavy burdens, and I will give you rest.*
> *Matthew 11:28-30*

The Magi would have welcomed this word of encouragement from Jesus. Little did they know, as they journeyed to the star, that the baby whose birth it proclaimed would indeed be the source of refreshment, the creator of the universe.

We're on a journey with the Magi these days. We come bearing gifts, setting out in haste, seeking the light. We have gifts for others, and the gifts we have been given by God in our talents and desires. We're in a hurry; there's not much time before the baby arrives!

Those wise men of long ago were most likely burdened in their travels by supplies, tents, necessities and luxuries for the road. But perhaps the greatest burden was understanding why they began this extraordinary search in the first place. With only their studies, and the light in the sky to guide them, they traveled in a kind of blind faith— confident that they must seek, but unsure of what their seeking will bring.

As we waver under the burdens of our busy lives, let's remember those desert wanderers centuries ago. While we may know who waits for us under the star, we too are searching for something new.

today I am grateful for

_____

_____

_____

my intentions for the day

_____

_____

_____

my to-do list for today

_____

_____

_____

_____

_____

_____

I will open rivers on the bare heights and fountains in the midst of valleys.
Isaiah 41:15

A spiritual mentor and friend once confided to me her frustration with how people pray: "We come to God with our buckets saying, 'Please fill these,' and God wants to give us the ocean!" God will never be outdone in generosity and creativity. Yet, we try to decide what's blessed for us, rather than letting God's blessings fill us.

There's an empty bucket in each of us. Blaise Pascal called it a "God shaped vacuum in the heart of every man which cannot be filled by any created thing, but only by God, the Creator, made known through Jesus."

Perhaps, when we pray, we're thinking too small. In your quiet time today, place your bucket of concerns before God. Imagine God's grace filling the bucket to overflowing, healing your concerns and bringing you peace of mind and heart. God is good. All is well.

today I am grateful for

_____

_____

my intentions for the day

_____

_____

_____

my to-do list for today

_____

_____

_____

_____

_____

_____

Happy are those who do not sit in the seat of scoffers.
Psalm 1:1

David begins the Book of Psalms with this clever admonishment. This is a tough one for me to follow, because I know a few scoffers, or cynics, and their wit entertains me immensely.

David, however, is touching on a deep truth about cynics. Cynicism is rooted in negativity and distrust. While a certain amount of cynicism is healthy, David warns us not to wallow in it if we truly seek happiness. The cynic's world view will assume the worst in a situation or person first, and may not be open to evidence to the contrary. As people of faith, viewing circumstances through the lens of God's love, we're called to a different outlook on life.

God loved us first, and called us into being. Trust that love, which is greater than all of creation. Find the goodness, and find happiness.

today I am grateful for

my intentions for the day

my to-do list for today

Restore us, O God; let your face shine, that we may be saved.
Psalm 80:4

We're bathed in Christmas lights. Whether tacky and extravagant or subdued and tasteful, the lights on display shine with the warmth and color of the season. The lights glimmer during the longest nights of the year, reassuring us that spring and summer are coming.

Last Christmas, we endured a powerful ice storm that knocked out power to tens of thousands of homes in our metropolitan area. The first day, we roughed it in our house, but as the temperature went down along with the sun, we were grateful to have shelter available at grandma's house. As we packed to leave, the house rapidly descended into darkness. It was nearly impossible to move around the house in ways we take for granted in the light of day.

Plunged into darkness, from a power outage or into life's dark passages, we long for the light. We trust and wait in hope.

Are you cursing the darkness these days? Find the glimmer of light within.

today I am grateful for _____

_____

_____

_____

my intentions for the day _____

_____

_____

_____

my to-do list for today _____

_____

_____

_____

_____

_____

_____

December 15

> *The Lord waits to be gracious to you; therefore he*
> *will rise up to show mercy to you.*
> *Isaiah 30:18*

The stress and anxiety of decking the halls can send us climbing the walls. Yet, the gifts, decorations and food we slave to prepare are really only faint shadows of the wonderful gifts God has given us in our talents, relationships and in creation.

Faith calls us to look at life through this lens: all is gift from God, and it's all pretty terrific, if we just pay attention! Faith gives us the opportunity to view ourselves, others, and life (even with all its stresses), as gift. Our concerns, joys and frustrations can be transformed.

This is the hope of Christmas. The baby born in Bethlehem brought life, innocence, potential and trust to a world hardened by death, deceit, suffering and broken dreams. Christmas means new beginnings, and hearts filled with hope.

In moments of longing or emptiness this season, remember to invite God into those feelings. God's love will provide the nourishment you truly need to sustain you today and the rest of this hectic and holy season.

today I am grateful for _____

_____

_____

_____

my intentions for the day _____

_____

_____

_____

my to-do list for today _____

_____

_____

_____

_____

_____

_____

December 16

Jesus said to them, "Let the little children come to me; do not stop them; for it is to such as these that the kingdom of God belongs."
Mark 10:14

Just before he spoke these words, the disciples had rebuked people for bringing their children to Jesus. One can imagine Jesus' handlers not wanting the Master to be bothered with messy, disruptive children. Instead, Jesus embraces them and dubs them owners of the great kingdom of God.

As he did so often, Jesus turned conventional wisdom on its side. The kingdom, the ultimate prize, will not go to the learned and accomplished, but to those who accept it like a child.

How often do we brush past a small child? In haste to get things done or go someplace, have we ignored our littlest ones? Done often enough, children get the message that whatever we're rushing to or busy about is more important than they are.

Today let the little children come to you. Embrace them and the precious gifts of laughter, insight and love they offer.

today I am grateful for

_____

_____

_____

my intentions for the day

_____

_____

_____

my to-do list for today

_____

_____

_____

_____

_____

_____

> *"Truly I tell you, whoever does not receive the kingdom of God as a little child will never enter it." Mark 10:15*

Children are terrific. They have some great characteristics that, if we emulate them, we'll be better prepared to enter the Kingdom of God.

Children are willing to dream. When our youngest was two, she sat on the bed with me, gently painting the air with my hair brush, saying, "Look, mom, I'm making a rainbow moon." Kids find the greatest potential in the simplest things.

Children are vulnerable, spontaneous and passionate. Kids express their feelings honestly. They live life fully engaged in the moment.

When Jesus says we must accept the Kingdom of God like a little child, he wants us to dream, open our hearts, and pay attention to what God has in store for us in every moment of life.

Play with your children or grandchildren today. Give them your undivided attention and have some fun. Or, recall a game or activity you liked as a child and spend at least 10 minutes doing it. Giggle when you want to giggle; find great potential in a simple thing. Create a Christmas Moment you'll want to recreate throughout the year.

today I am grateful for

my intentions for the day

my to-do list for today

"Are you the one who is to come, or are we to wait for another?"
Luke 7:20

John the Baptist sent two of his disciples to pose this question to Jesus. One can imagine the scene: They stand before this man who displays awesome power to heal. Scratching their heads, maybe nervously giggling a bit, they ask, "Is this for real? Do we trust you?"

These disciples showed a great child-like quality to Jesus—willing to be vulnerable, to ask the question, and perhaps more profoundly to stand open to the answer and the implications it held for their lives. Jesus asked them to watch, and report back to John what they had seen and heard. They would know him by his works, and believe.

What are the miracles you've experienced in your life? How did they change you? Is your heart open for a miracle this season?

today I am grateful for _____

_____

_____

my intentions for the day _____

_____

_____

_____

my to-do list for today _____

_____

_____

_____

_____

_____

_____

With everlasting love I will have compassion on you.
Isaiah 54:8

The holidays can be the loneliest time of the year. Movies and songs leave us wishing for a companion to share it with, or remembering those with whom we shared the holidays in days past.

Before I was married, I wanted someone special in my life at the holidays. After marriage, my husband and I negotiated between our individual expectations of the holidays, from where we'd spend our time with our respective families, to divvying up tasks around the house. The first Christmas after my dad died, I had the hardest time getting into the spirit.

All these experiences showed me how important it is to be in touch with my own heart and soul throughout the holidays. Our souls are our connection to God, the one from whom our lives have come. Reconnecting with God throughout the day helps keep that line open, and the creeping loneliness at bay.

Is there someone you've been meaning to spend some time with, or would like to get to know better? Meet for a quick cup of coffee. Delight in this unexpected gift of companionship during these days of preparation.

today I am grateful for

my intentions for the day

my to-do list for today

December 20

To you, O Lord, I lift up my soul. O my God, in you I trust.
Psalm 25:1-2

This passage brings forth a vision of a tired, harried woman throwing her arms to the sky, imploring God for help. She's surrounded by dirty laundry, hungry children, a ringing phone, and streams of ribbon and glitter spilled on the floor.

She's stretched, all right. We're in the home stretch, the last few days leading up to the glory of Christmas Day. Perhaps you are beginning to negotiate with your to-do list—choosing now to forgo sleep and food in order to accomplish it all, or you're moving projects to the "maybe next year" category.

Your thoughts are too focused on the *stuff* again. Set it all aside. Open your arms and let the glorious savior in. Don't remain locked by your determination to get it all done. Let the savior carry things for a while.

today I am grateful for

_____

_____

_____

my intentions for the day

_____

_____

_____

my to-do list for today

_____

_____

_____

_____

_____

_____

_____

For as soon as I heard your greeting, the child in my womb leaped for joy.
Luke 1:44

Mary and Elizabeth: a holy friendship, gifted with holy intuition.

Do you have an Elizabeth in your life? A dear friend you can run to and pour out your heart? One who sees, affirms and is uplifted by the goodness she sees in you?

Mary's intuition to visit Elizabeth was right on. She discovered her cousin was with child, too. They had so much to share. Elizabeth affirmed in Mary the life she carried in her womb.

Surround yourself with the Elizabeths in your life. Affirm and support each other's goodness. Include your Elizabeths on your gratitude list today.

today I am grateful for

_____

_____

_____

my intentions for the day

_____

_____

_____

my to-do list for today

_____

_____

_____

_____

_____

_____

Mary said, "My soul magnifies the Lord, and my spirit rejoices in God my Savior, for he has looked with favor on the lowliness of his servant. Surely from now on all generations will call me blessed; for the Mighty one has done great things for me, and holy is his name."
Luke 1:46

We mistake humility as pushing aside our strengths, beauty or accomplishments. Someone compliments us, and we deny the compliment. "It was nothing." "This old thing?" "I got it on sale." On and on.

Mary models true humility to us—she acknowledges her blessings, and gives God all the credit. She doesn't deny her gifts, but rejoices in them as if to say, "Look at me! Isn't this great? Is God awesome, or what?"

Let's follow Mary's example once again. First of all, a simple "Thank you" is sufficient for most compliments. Secondly, when we recognize gifts in ourselves, instead of denying them, thank and praise God for them. And finally, don't be afraid to share your gifts with others.

Today, spend a few minutes doing something you're really good at and delight in doing. Let that chuckle of delight rise from your heart. Praise God, for you are wonderfully made!

today I am grateful for _____

_____

_____

_____

my intentions for the day _____

_____

_____

_____

_____

my to-do list for today _____

_____

_____

_____

_____

_____

_____

_____

*And you, child, shall be called the prophet of the Most High; for
you will go before the Lord to prepare his ways, to give knowledge of
salvation to his people by the forgiveness of their sins.*
Luke 1:76-77

John the Baptist played a marvelous role in salvation history. Jesus
showed the way to salvation, and John turned people's attention to
Jesus. "Repent, for the kingdom of heaven is at hand!" (Matthew 3: 2)
John lived an authentic life; he did what he was born to do.

Each of us has a part to play in continuing Jesus' work on earth. We
are uniquely blessed with talents to be celebrated, developed, and
directed to service for God. In the classic movie, *Chariots of Fire*, the
great runner Eric Liddell was torn between his call to the Christian
missions and his passion for running. He understood his authentic life
by the joy he experienced when using his talents. Eric became an
Olympic gold medalist *and* served as a missionary in China; he
honored his gifts and gave glory to God in the process.

God, help me to recognize and develop my talents. Help me to
glorify you by living an authentic life.

today I am grateful for —————————————

———————————————————————

———————————————————————

———————————————————————

my intentions for the day ————————————

———————————————————————

———————————————————————

———————————————————————

my to-do list for today ——————————————

———————————————————————

———————————————————————

———————————————————————

———————————————————————

———————————————————————

———————————————————————

December 24

*Suddenly there was with the angel a multitude of the
heavenly host, praising God and saying, "Glory to God in the
highest heaven, and on earth peace!"*
Luke 2:13-14

A Christmas Moment! What a spectacle! There were the shepherds,
just doing their job, when suddenly legions of God's finest filled
the skies with news of Jesus' birth.

The anticipation of Christmas fills our hearts this day. Children
await the treasures of Christmas morning; adults know that these weeks
of preparation are about to come to fruition. The babe is about to be
born.

For children the time passes too slowly, but adults have learned the
sweetness of waiting. For a few moments tonight, when the house is
dark, sit in silence by the lighted Christmas tree. Take a deep breath
and close your eyes. Do you remember the tree from your childhood
home? Can you smell the delicious foods being prepared for the feast?
As a child, did you listen for sleigh bells, lying awake in the night? Ah,
the joys of anticipation!

Now look at your Christmas lights. Let your eyes soak in the
warmth and color. Imagine the shepherds, as they gazed up at the sky,
slowly comprehending the meaning of the angels' appearance. As you
look forward to the day ahead, give thanks to God for his gifts of joy,
anticipation, and this annual opportunity to relive it all.

today I am grateful for _____

_____

_____

_____

my intentions for the day _____

_____

_____

_____

my to-do list for today _____

_____

_____

_____

_____

_____

_____

When the angels had left them and gone into heaven, the shepherds said to one another, "Let us go now to Bethlehem and see this thing that has taken place, which the Lord has made known to us." So they went with haste and found Mary and Joseph, and the child lying in the manger. When they saw this, they made known what had been told them about this child; and all who heard it were amazed at what the shepherds told them. But Mary treasured all these words and pondered them in her heart. The shepherds returned, praising God for all they had heard and seen.
Luke 2: 15-20

Amen!

There's no to-do list on the next page. Today join the shepherds and write prayers of praise and thanksgiving.

Christmas Season

Bear with one another, and, if anyone has a complaint against another, forgive each other just as the Lord has forgiven you. Above all, clothe yourselves with love, which binds everything together in perfect harmony.
Colossians 3:13-14

Today might be a let down, as often happens after a big event like Christmas. The weeks of preparation are done. The packages opened, the food eaten. The house falls quiet with a much-needed sigh of relief.

As you look back on the day, do you have any regrets? Anything you wish you'd said or done differently? Take a moment to think of the circumstances, and the people involved. Then gently say a prayer for each one—and let go of your regrets. God knows what happened, and what's in your heart. You can't change what happened, but you can love more fully next time.

Today, don't dwell on the regrets. Turn your thoughts to the Christmas Moments you've experienced with people you love. These joys are what you worked so hard to bring to life. Give thanks for the contribution you made to theirs, and your own, great Christmas.

today I am grateful for

_____

_____

_____

my intentions for the day

_____

_____

_____

my to-do list for today

_____

_____

_____

_____

_____

_____

Christmas Season

This life was revealed, and we have seen it and testified to it, and declare to you the eternal life that was with the Father and was revealed to us. We are writing these things so that your joy may be complete.
1 John 1:2, 4

Jesus is the human face of God. After centuries of signs and wonders to the people of the Old Testament, God revealed himself to humanity in the person of Jesus Christ, the beautiful boy in the manger. All who saw him shared their joy with others, so they too would know his wonder.

This year, our daily reflection and gratitude practice have shown us the wonder of Jesus in new ways. The stories, music and traditions we share every year have taken on added meaning.

Page through this book and reread some of your gratitude lists, intentions and to-do lists. Do you find any new insights? How was God made visible to you during Advent? Give thanks for these, and for all you accomplished preparing for a great Christmas.

today I am grateful for

_____

my intentions for the day

my to-do list for today

> *We have escaped like a bird from the snare of the fowlers.*
> Psalm 124:7

Celebrate! We are freed from the burdens of Christmas preparations. The anticipation, the preparations for the big day have all come to an end. The day that loomed so large for so long is now past. We're heading into a new year with memories of another Christmas feast.

Imagine Mary gazing at her baby, Jesus. She, too, is freed from the confines of pregnancy; freed to care for this new life entrusted to her. The long-awaited child just arrived, and yet the memory of a time without him is already slipping from her mind.

The New Year for many is a time to reevaluate priorities and set new goals. A good way to identify your goals might be to consider: For what purpose, what new life, have you been freed this Advent season?

today I am grateful for _____

_____

_____

my intentions for the day _____

_____

_____

my to-do list for today _____

_____

_____

_____

_____

_____

For the darkness is over and the real light begins to shine.
1 John 2:7

A popular bumper sticker proclaims: "S*** HAPPENS." Perhaps the better perspective is "LOVE HAPPENS."

Life is a combination of the two. "Life is difficult," writes M. Scott Peck in his classic, *The Road Less Traveled*. Once we accept this truth, he says, then life is no longer difficult.

Our perspective on life has everything to do with our expectations. If we expect life to be care-free, then when the difficulties arise, we feel we have been treated unfairly. Focus on the bad things and after a while, that's all we'll see.

Jesus was born at a time in history no less turbulent than our own. He brought unconditional love and unfailing hope to the world. For those of us who carry the title "Christian," that responsibility is ours today … right down to the bumper stickers we put on our cars.

What are the signs of hope and love you see in your life today? How can you spread the good news that "LOVE HAPPENS"?

today I am grateful for —————————

———————————————

———————————————

———————————————

my intentions for the day —————————

———————————————

———————————————

———————————————

my to-do list for today —————————

———————————————

———————————————

———————————————

———————————————

———————————————

———————————————

> *The child grew and became strong, filled with*
> *wisdom; and the favor of God was upon him.*
> Luke 2:40

Our Bible tells us very little about the years between Jesus' childhood and the start of his public ministry. This quote is like a movie montage that gives the viewer a sense of time's passage, and how the main character grows or changes during that time.

There's a reassuring quality to this passage as well. Imagine Jesus in his home with his parents, performing his expected chores and learning carpentry from Joseph. He was, undoubtedly, an insightful and bright child, with wisdom beyond his years.

The passage comes at the right time in the Christmas season. Following the festivities of the holidays, we may be longing to return to our normal schedule. Life is always hectic, of course, but some times of the year are more hectic than others. Certainly the holidays are at the top of the list. This passage's glimpse into the life of Jesus reminds us of the comforts of everyday life, and that God's grace is working in our lives even on the most ordinary of days.

At the end of this church season, we'll return to "ordinary time." Think about some of the ways ordinary time holds hidden blessings for you. What are the ways you find God present in the midst of your daily life?

today I am grateful for _____

_____

_____

_____

my intentions for the day _____

_____

_____

_____

my to-do list for today _____

_____

_____

_____

_____

_____

_____

Christmas Season

Of his fullness we have all had a share—love following upon love.
John 1:17

As the calendar year draws to a close, today is an ideal time to reflect on the last twelve months and identify your:

- Accomplishments;
- Setbacks;
- Surprises;
- Celebrations.

So much living goes on in the days and weeks that seem to fly by! During your quiet time today, use your calendar to remind you of all that has transpired this year. Give thanks for the gift of one more year of life!

today I am grateful for

_____

_____

_____

my intentions for the day

_____

_____

_____

my to-do list for today

_____

_____

_____

_____

_____

_____

New Year's Day

Rejoice in the Lord always; again I will say, rejoice. Let your gentleness be known to everyone. The Lord is near. Do not worry about anything, but in everything by prayer and supplication with thanksgiving let your requests be made known to God. And the peace of God, which surpasses all understanding, will guard your hearts and your minds in Christ Jesus.
Philippians 4:4-6

Happy New Year! We see these words everywhere and repeat them to everyone this time of year. Like any other phrase that's overused, it has lost some of its meaning. Is it really a new year? And will it be happy?

Although the calendar page has turned to a new year, we may still be living in the last one. What old habits or beliefs do we carry with us? Are they helping us grow, or are they holding us back from God's glorious dream for our lives? If we changed some of these old habits, would our lives be happier, more fulfilling?

Today's scripture passage offers a great formula for a Happy New Year:

- Rejoice in the Lord.
- Thank God for everything.
- Be gentle with others and yourself.
- Don't worry about anything.
- Trust God with all your concerns.

If we set our mind and heart to these admonitions everyday, we'll know real peace.

today I am grateful for

_____

_____

_____

my intentions for the day

_____

_____

_____

my to-do list for today

_____

_____

_____

_____

_____

_____

_____

> *Finally, beloved, whatever is true, whatever is honorable,*
> *whatever is just, whatever is pure, whatever is pleasing, whatever is*
> *commendable, if there is any excellence, and if there is anything*
> *worthy of praise, think about these things.*
> *Philippians 4:8*

Think about good things. Too often, our thoughts drift to recounting our transgressions or replaying scenes of conflict, searching for the perfect retort—the "I wish I would have said …" comment that would influence our opponents.

Or we live waiting for the proverbial "other shoe" to drop. Recently, I remarked to an acquaintance about the weather on a particularly beautiful day. He responded, "Yeah, if only it'd stay this way." As soon as good things happen, we brace ourselves for the next bad thing to come along.

St. Paul proposes a different mindset. Instead of focusing on what isn't working, waiting for the next bad thing to happen, he suggests we turn our attention to what is working. What is working is evidence of the kingdom in our midst. Paul describes a vision of heaven, and it's exciting to realize there's proof of it in our world.

For today, pay attention to your thoughts. When they slip to the negative, or you find yourself replaying a difficult scene in your mind, stop. Turn your attention to something good or worthwhile in the situation, and focus on that. Be sure to pray for those you're in conflict with; it is remarkable how God's grace will release the tension when you do.

today I am grateful for _____

_____

_____

my intentions for the day _____

_____

_____

_____

my to-do list for today _____

_____

_____

_____

_____

_____

_____

Christmas Season

*I pray that the God of our Lord Jesus Christ may give you a spirit
of wisdom and revelation as you come to know him, so that, with the
eyes of your heart enlightened, you may know … the immeasurable
greatness of his power for us who believe. God put this power to work in
Christ when he raised him from the dead.*
Ephesians 1:17-20

The same power that raised Christ from the dead, at work in your
life! Imagine!

The immeasurable greatness of his power. The creator of the universe
is active in your life. God has dreamed a dream for you, a dream that's
in your soul, the blueprint of which is in your talents. We have each
been uniquely blessed with a certain set of skills and talents, born to
this particular family at this time in history. We each have our work to
do, and if we don't do it, the work will go undone.

For us who believe. Of course, we believe in God, but do we really
believe God has a great dream for our lives? Do we believe in God's
abundant generosity and creativity to bring our dreams into reality?
When we truly believe, life takes on meaning and direction.

God has given us a clue to his dream for us in the talents we've
been given. This year, explore the talents that engage you passionately.
The joy that comes in developing these talents is evidence of God's
presence in them. Joseph Campbell advises, "Follow your bliss and
don't be afraid, and doors will open where you didn't know they were
going to be." Trust in God. Remember, the power of the resurrection is
at work in you!

today I am grateful for

_____

_____

_____

my intentions for the day

_____

_____

_____

my to-do list for today

_____

_____

_____

_____

_____

_____

> *A bruised reed he will not break, and a dimly*
> *burning wick he will not quench.*
> *Isaiah 42:3*

One misconception that comes with finding your passion in life is that, once we find it, we'll never do work we find boring or have a bad day again. Wrong.

There are those who view how easily things come to them as confirmation that they are on the right track. If projects become difficult or obstacles appear, they assume they made the wrong choice somewhere along the line. This path must not be God's will for their lives, they say, or things would be so much easier.

Jesus said, "In the world you face persecution. But take courage; I have conquered the world!" (John 16:33) Challenges are a part of life, not a measure of our proximity to God.

When we're blessed to do work that draws on our talents and passions, the work is still demanding. Plus, living out of our passion is no reprieve from other commitments. So there is always the struggle to honor those commitments and the work God has called us to do. Sometimes they are one and the same.

If a dark day comes this year, when you're wondering if you're on the right track, take a moment of quiet prayer and bring your concerns to God. God's love will heal your bruised soul, and fan into flame your spirit.

today I am grateful for

_____

_____

_____

my intentions for the day

_____

_____

_____

my to-do list for today

_____

_____

_____

_____

_____

_____

> *Let us love, not in word or speech, but in truth and action.*
> *1 John 3:18*

"It is no use walking anywhere to preach unless our walking is our preaching." *St. Francis of Assisi*

This admonition, from scripture and St. Francis, is one of the most deeply challenging in the Christian life. We aspire to live a life that reflects the love Jesus showed those around him, but when it comes right down to it, he set the bar pretty high.

Walking the walk starts with talking the talk. Go to church, read spiritual materials, and spend time with people who share your values; you'll meet them at church, work, or down the street. It's important to be around people with whom you can discuss your spiritual journey. They'll uphold the choices you make, and give gentle guidance when you need direction. All these activities will nourish and strengthen you.

Now comes the hard part: *walking the walk.* Everyday we have opportunities to show our beliefs in the choices we make. How we relate to family members and those we encounter throughout the day, for starters. Business decisions we make, civic or political organizations we support, volunteer work, and entertainment venues we patronize all reflect our core values. Will those we encounter see our enthusiasm—the God within—and want to emulate it in their own lives? Or will they see someone who's just talking?

today I am grateful for _____

_____

_____

my intentions for the day _____

_____

_____

_____

my to-do list for today _____

_____

_____

_____

_____

_____

_____

> *There, ahead of them, went the star that they had seen at its rising,*
> *until it stopped over the place where the child was. When they saw*
> *that the star had stopped, they were overwhelmed with joy. On entering*
> *the house, they saw the child with Mary his mother; and they knelt down*
> *and paid him homage. Then, opening their treasure chests, they offered*
> *him gifts of gold, frankincense and myrrh.*
> *Matthew 2:9-11*

We have come to the end of our journey. Like the Magi, we have traveled in faith, to places unknown, following the light. We carried our burdens, our gifts, all with the unfailing hope that our journey would prove worthwhile. New insights and newfound peace during the holidays were our destination. We have shared the Magi's joy of finally arriving at that destination. When they beheld the Christ, their hearts were filled to overflowing with joy; they poured out their gifts to this mother and child, so overjoyed were they to have arrived.

T.S. Eliot writes, "The end of all our exploring will be to arrive where we started and to know it for the first time." For the Magi, perhaps there was the sense of coming home of which Eliot speaks. For us, we may not have traveled far physically, but we have journeyed within, our steps opening a path for God's Holy Spirit to enter and love, heal and bring peace to our hearts. Returning to this place, where we started, we truly know it for the first time, having been transformed by the power of God.

today I am grateful for ───────────────

──────────────────────────────

──────────────────────────────

my intentions for the day ───────────────

──────────────────────────────

──────────────────────────────

my to-do list for today ───────────────

──────────────────────────────

──────────────────────────────

──────────────────────────────

──────────────────────────────

──────────────────────────────

additional journal pages

Acknowledgments

My heartfelt thanks go out to the wonderful people who helped bring this book into being:

Lisa Hinrichs (www.lisahinrichsdesigns.com) for her beautiful design;

Julie Hood (www.juliehood.com) and the members of our mastermind group for their marketing expertise and encouragement;

Mary Menke (www.wordabilities.com) for her editing skills;

Bob Baker (www.Bob-Baker.com) and the St. Louis Publishers Association for guidance in the publishing process;

The Women of Holy Infant Parish (Ballwin, Missouri) and St. Peter's Parish (St. Charles, Missouri), for repeatedly welcoming me to their Advent gatherings;

The Staff and Retreatants of King's House, Belleville, Illinois, for helping me find my voice;

Renee Bauer Soffer and Rainey Fahey for their love and encouragement;

Steve, my husband and best friend, for his unfailing belief in me and my talent;

Abby and Katie, my daughters, who love Christmas as much as I do.

Prepare Your Heart for a Great Christmas!

To order books, visit with other women on the Advent journey, and discover resources for creating Christmas Moments, visit **www.GreatChristmasBook.com**.

Maria Rodgers O'Rourke's heartfelt perspectives on Advent and Christmas make for popular presentations to women's organizations. To invite Maria to speak to your group, visit **www.GreatChristmasBook.com**.

Order your copy for next year!
Prepare Your Heart for a Great Christmas is published by
MRO Communications, Inc.
1602 Fontana Drive, St. Louis, Missouri, 63146
Phone: 314-359-1942
Contact **orders@GreatChristmasBook.com** for more information.